HOW TO START A SUCCESSFUL RESTAURANT

HOW TO START A SUCCESSFUL RESTAURANT

An Entrepreneur's Guide

James J. Breen
William D. Sanderson

Lebhar-Friedman Books
Chain Store Publishing Corp.
A Subsidiary of Lebhar-Friedman Inc.
New York

Library of Congress Cataloging in Publication Data:
Breen, James J.
    How to start a successful restaurant.

    Bibliography: p.
    Includes index.
    1. Restaurant management. I. Sanderson, William D. II. Title.
TX911.3.M27B73   647'.95'068   81-18089
ISBN 0-86730-242-9   AACR2

5   4   3   2   1

This book is dedicated to the Breen and Sanderson families whose inspiration and encouragement have guided us in creating this tool so that it might inspire and encourage other entrepreneurs.

CONTENTS

CHAPTER FOUR
Other Topics of Importance

Accounting Systems • Advertising • Buying an Existing Business • Buying a Franchise • Equipment • Facilities • Financing • Insurance • Inventory Control • Job Descriptions • Leases—Common Terminology • Legal Forms of Organization • Liquor Licenses • Location • Management Information and Control Systems • Market Research • Permits, Taxes, and Registrations • Personnel • Planning and Timing • Policies and Procedures • Security • Using Professional Services Effectively • Trade Associations • Trade Journals • Suggested Readings

PREFACE

All persons interested in starting their own restaurants, expanding or improving an existing operations, or becoming passive investors in restaurant ventures, will find *How to Start a Successful Restaurant* an invaluable tool in developing, planning, and executing their ideas.

This book was developed to give the proper advice, guidance, and direction to individuals who wish to venture on their own into the highly competitive and complex restaurant business. Many restaurant operations are extremely profitable while others fail miserably. Our purpose is to make your venture a profitable one. This guide will give you the edge over your competition and save you a tremendous amount of time and money in the process.

Essentially this book will act as a planning tool to orchestrate your ideas into a successful and profitable restaurant operation. In a clear and concise fashion, all the essential ingredients of a professional business proposal will be illustrated in the chapters ahead. In addition to planning advice, advice is given on selecting the various necessary services, such as lawyers, accountants, and banks, as well as dealing with them effectively.

This guide will walk you through the complex and multi-faceted tasks of the restaurant entrepreneur with the intention of smoothing the development process, reducing your costs, minimizing the risks, and thus improving the probability of success.

James J. Breen
William D. Sanderson
1981

CHAPTER ONE

GETTING STARTED

The only way to realize your restaurant dream is to organize your efforts and thoughts around a solid conceptual foundation. There are two basic ways to begin your operation and both have to do with marketing. One is to develop a sound concept or restaurant type and then choose a market in which it would best fit. The second way is to take a choice location and create a restaurant to suit the needs of that market.

THE CONCEPT APPROACH

Many entrepreneurs have been creating dream restaurants in their minds for years. Others have been studying the market closely and feel that a certain type of restaurant will succeed at a particular time. Still others have a special recipe or an idea for a unique theme. Each of these ideas can build a foundation for further development. Once the conceptual foundation has been established, all further efforts should revolve around it. The next logical step would be to find a location in which this concept would be most successful. This will be covered in the next section.

LOCATION APPROACH

There are many locations and geographical areas that can be potential gold mines for the observant individual. Basically the location approach to beginning a restaurant is studying the area that you think would make a good location for a restaurant to determine if a restaurant is needed in that particular area. Common high-potential areas are large shopping malls, heavily trafficked areas, sites with particularly good vistas, or busy business districts. Wherever the consumer's desire to dine out is unfulfilled, you have a potential site for a restaurant. After studying the potential location thoroughly, if you are convinced that the demand for an eating establishment is real, develop a concept that can best satisfy the demand.

A GOOD LOCATION OR CONCEPT

As you can see, it is important to adopt one approach or the other to be on your way toward starting your own restaurant or expanding current operations. A prime location or a good concept will give you the necessary foundation for accomplishing your goal. One approach, however, is not necessarily better than the other. The most successful restaurants combine a good location with a good concept. One without the other will generally not suffice.

Now that you understand the two marketing concepts, and have presumably chosen one, the rest of the guide will serve as a model for developing it. As we continue through the business plan, your dream will take shape in reality.

WHAT IS THE RESTAURANT BUSINESS PROPOSAL?

The business proposal or plan serves many purposes. First of all, it is a plan of action. The proposal depicts the restaurant's concept and its goals, as well as the tactics and strategies for meeting your goals. The proposal is also a sales document. It is designed to give credibility to both the idea and the management team. It must convey confidence and excitement in order to *induce* the investor to invest in what he feels will be the next McDonald's, Denny's, or Beefsteak Charlie's.

WHAT IS THE PURPOSE OF A PROPOSAL?

The purpose of the proposal can vary greatly from a simple management plan to a document used to procure millions of dollars in financing. No matter what the purpose, all proposals should contain essentially the same elements. Most importantly the proposal should show how your restaurant will exhibit three key characteristics:

1. A proprietory product in a growing industry
2. An outstanding management team
3. A unique market niche

WHAT DOES A RESTAURANT BUSINESS PROPOSAL CONTAIN?

An outline of the elements of a restaurant business proposal appears in Table 1. Depending on the concept, different sections of the proposal will be emphasized to a greater or lesser degree. The total length of the proposal should not exceed 20 to 25 pages (excluding exhibits). A very lengthy proposal could turn off potential investors; the idea is to keep it short and exciting, with each section leading to the next, creating a feeling of anticipation.

In Chapter Two, each aspect of the proposal will be discussed and outlined in detail.

TABLE 1

The Restaurant Business Proposal
Outline

1. Plan Summary
2. Management Team
3. Restaurant Concept
4. Customer Profile
5. Location
6. Competition
7. Marketing Plan
8. Organization and Personnel
9. Operations
10. Growth Strategy
11. Financial Plan
12. Industry Survey

CHAPTER TWO

THE RESTAURANT BUSINESS PROPOSAL

PLAN SUMMARY

The summary is sometimes called the executive summary, mini-proposal, or introduction. It serves as a brief introduction that summarizes the plan. If the plan is designed to obtain financing, it explains how much is needed, what it will be used for, and how it will be paid back. The summary should be exciting and fulfill the following objectives:

1. gain the investor's interest
2. inspire him or her to read the remainder of the proposal
3. develop investor confidence in the concept
4. illustrate the potential of the idea.

Keep the summary short. Some investors read many business plans each month, and a lengthy, wordy proposal will quickly lose the investor's attention.

Remember, the summary should be detailed enough to discuss all the highlights, well-written enough to communicate confidence, and brief enough to invite curiosity and induce action.

5

THE MANAGEMENT TEAM

This section of the proposal is considered the most important by many investors. Why a management team? Today's sophisticated investors are reluctant to invest in a one-man show. In such a dynamic business environment, it is difficult for one man to wear all the hats. Typically, each key management discipline should be covered by someone who has demonstrated exceptional capability in his/her previous experiences.

The key management positions should be described in terms of duties and responsibilities. Then the respective management members should be tied to each position, illustrating his/her capability by citing past experience and accomplishments. The résumés of the team members should appear in the appendix. If personal guarantees are needed for loans, the personal balance sheets of the management team should also appear in the appendix.

THE RESTAURANT CONCEPT

Describing the restaurant concept can be the biggest selling point of the entire proposal. There are two basic areas which should be detailed to make this section come alive. One is the restaurant's motif and the other is its cuisine.

In describing the motif, the object is to involve the reader in the atmosphere, mood, and surroundings of the restaurant as graphically as possible. Reading the description, one should be able to "experience" the restaurant and feel as if one is actually there. Singular characteristics should be highlighted. Why is this particular restaurant unique? What makes it better than others? This section should appeal to people's emotions as well as their senses.

The cuisine should be described succinctly, but again, with the singular characteristics highlighted. Perhaps the food preparation or presentation is unique. Possibly the menu caters to one group or another. Explain why the concept is a good idea. Of course each restaurant will have unique features, many of which may deviate from the illustration in this guide. In the restaurant business, *vive la différence* is the creed.

CUSTOMER PROFILE

A very important body of information commonly overlooked is the customer profile. After developing your concept, determine who your customer is and where he or she is located. Decide whether your particular concept has wide appeal or caters to a small group of people.

This section of the proposal should depict the typical customer. Descriptive data should include age, sex, annual income, marital status, size of family, and level of education.

LOCATION

This section of the proposal should be used to describe the location of the unit and justify its selection.

Location is a key element of your total business plan. Too often, not enough thought is given to such an important decision. Data that should be collected in order to make an intelligent decision about site location include:

- competition
- traffic count
- the types of businesses nearby (are they good generators of potential customers?)
- peak hours of traffic
- plans for growth in the area
- availability of public transportation
- parking facilities and ease of access
- the destinations of passers-by
- the number of residents within a given radius of the location
- visibility from adjacent stores

- the average sales of competitors in the area
- other demographic data which is considered unique to your location.

Your local real-estate agent or leasing agent can be of great assistance. They maintain up-to-date lists of available sites and demographic data on the area. Other sources of information include the market research department of local newspapers, the chamber of commerce, the city planning office, and the local library.

COMPETITION

Use this section of the proposal to analyze the competition and assess your competitive advantages and disadvantages.

A matrix format is often used in this section. Table 2 illustrates a sample matrix that would be appropriate. Of course, the characteristics that are used in comparison will vary depending on the type of restaurant and the competition.

Other competitive factors which you may want to consider include: view, wine and beer or full bar, quality, location, independent or chain, etc.

THE MARKETING PLAN

Effective marketing programs do not just happen—they are planned. The dynamic nature and complexity of our economy, combined with stiff competition and rising labor and food costs, make effective planning essential for success. A good marketing plan and its implementation require advance scheduling, uncover problem areas early enough to be corrected, use administrative time effectively, improve communication and coordination, and thus increase the potential for achieving company goals. The plan should contain three elements: (1) a statement of marketing objectives; (2) a description of the specific means to achieve the objective; and (3) a planning time period (horizon) with a schedule of events.

TABLE 2

Assessment of Competitive Advantages and Disadvantages

Name	Fish Fantasy	Johnny D's	Lobster Haven	Hawaiian Palace
Menu	Limited Seafood	Prime Rib	Seafood	Steak/ Seafood
Price	Medium	Medium	Medium	High
Hours	11 am- 11 pm	11 am- 12 am	5 pm- 12 am	5 pm- 12 am
Credit Cards Accepted	Master Card, Visa	None	Master Card, Visa	American Express, Master Card, Visa, Diners Club

Customers

Although you may feel your restaurant will appeal to many types of people, you should be able to describe the customer base and its characteristics. This is sometimes referred to as a customer profile. For example, you may be located in an area with many office buildings and industrial complexes and concentrate on the business-man's lunch. Or you may be located in an area with many single family dwellings and consider your operation a family restaurant.

Demographic data can tell you a lot about a potential market, and this can be matched with your strategy. However, today you must be aware of much more than the number of people in an area, how much money they earn, and how many children they have. You must also be aware of social changes, trends, economic conditions, and other such variables. Keep in mind:

- We are migrating from northern industrial areas to warmer climate areas.
- More and more married women are continuing to work or returning to work.
- The median age is approaching thirty-five, as we become a society of adults.
- The consumption of beef and coffee is down while the consumption of fish and tea is up.

All of these factors should be examined closely in determining a concept and the type of customer that will patronize your establishment. But remember, change is a continuing phenomenon. Be aware, be flexible, and be receptive to such change.

Product

This section of the proposal explains the menu and the products offered (a sample menu should appear in the appendix). Beware of menu monotony. The menu and its make-up can be a powerful marketing tool. It is a major link between you and your guests and should be used to its greatest potential. The menu should be well-balanced, well-organized, and easy to read. Don't be afraid to try new recipes as "specials" or to change the menu periodically. As in any other business, customers' tastes change and you will have to be flexible with your product mix (menu mix) in order to satisfy your customers' needs.

Generally, the larger the selection, the easier it is to obtain a balanced menu. However, with rising labor costs and increasing food and energy costs, many operations are limiting their selections to reduce inventory, kitchen size, and food waste. This can easily lead to an unbalanced menu. Be careful not to limit your menu in such a way that you severely limit your potential market. If a limited menu is utilized, periodic reviews of each menu item are very important.

Pricing

Outline your pricing policy in this section. Be sure your policy is consistent with your desired image or character. If you wish to convey the image of high quality and exceptional service, your pricing policy should be consistent with this image.

Although there are many different ways to price a menu, the authors recommend a simple yet valuable method known as prime costing.

The increased use of foods that are partially or completely prepared outside the kitchen has changed the way restaurateurs are pricing their menus. Food items prepared outside the operator's unit decrease in-house labor costs. Using the prime cost method, food cost and direct labor cost are combined and labeled "prime." Now the "prime" cost includes part of the total labor.

Table 3 illustrates an example of "prime" costing a seafood dinner.

The multiplier will vary from restaurant to restaurant and from item to item. Other factors will affect picking a multiplier:

1. Cost fluctuations throughout the year
2. Competition's prices
3. Volume of item sold
4. Customers' sensitivity to changing prices (price elasticity of demand)
5. Perishability
6. Cost of carrying an item in inventory
7. Gross profit needed to cover operating expenses

Promotion and Advertising

The amount of money allocated to advertising and promotion expenditures can vary from zero to six percent of sales. In this section, outline and justify the budget, and present the advertising

TABLE 3

Prime Costing

	6 oz. Cod Filet	4 oz. Steamed Vegetable	Baked Potato
Food Cost	$0.95	$ 0.14	$0.08
+ Prepared Labor Cost	—	0.105	0.02
+ Pre-prepared Added Direct Labor (Cooks)	0.09	0.05	0.05
= Prime Cost	1.04	0.295	0.15
× Multiplier (3) =	$3.12	$0.885	$0.45

Dinner Price:
6 oz. Cod Filet	$3.12
4 oz. Steamed Vegetable	0.88
Baked Potato	0.45
Menu Price	$4.45

promotion campaign plan. Where will the dollars go and what are the desired results? Again, this plan should be consistent with the restaurant's image and be in tune with the competition's practices.

Advertising includes dollars spent on newspaper ads, radio, television, magazines, billboards, and mailers. Promotion includes contests, shows, and gift certificates.

ORGANIZATION AND PERSONNEL

Certainly the restaurant business is a people business. Good personnel is an effective marketing tool and can shape the character of a restaurant.

There are certain considerations which the entrepreneur must be aware of in this area.

Define Personnel Needs

Labor can be a very costly item, ranging from fifteen to thirty-five percent of sales, depending on the type of establishment. Therefore, care must be taken to accurately forecast the personnel needs of the restaurant. Much can be learned by observing competitors or similar establishments. Ask experts in the field. At any rate, this is a critical factor to be considered. Effective and efficient layout of equipment and fixtures can save a large amount of labor over the years. This area is discussed later and deserves a great deal of attention.

Estimate Labor Hour Usage

Perhaps the best way to determine what personnel needs will be is to first estimate the number of labor hours needed. Because many staffs consist of part-time help, knowing how many labor hours will be needed is more realistic than estimating numbers of personnel. Once this is determined, full-time and/or part-time help can be hired to meet the expected labor requirements.

Organization Structure

In this section of the business plan, plot each position and task, and outline the authority and responsibility hierarchy. Well-defined job descriptions reduce uncertainty on the parts of both employees and management. The less the duties overlap and the better the lines of supervision are defined, the smoother the restaurant will run. Because a restaurant is so labor intensive, it is essential that all job descriptions are well detailed and understood by employees.

OPERATIONS

This section of the plan should describe the backbone of the restaurant—the equipment to be used, workflow of the staff, and sources of supply for equipment and food.

GROWTH STRATEGY

Long-Term Goals: Most entrepreneurs have long-range goals for their restaurants. Some want to build the most spectacular restaurant around. Others want to gain a reputation for good food at low or medium prices. Still others want to build their concept into a chain of restaurants. Defining your goals in the business proposal is the best start toward achieving them.

Five-Year Plan: Begin by determining where you want your establishment to be in five years. Three of the most common goals are:

1. To increase unit sales
2. To expand to additional units
3. To diversify existing unit.

Keep your goals firmly in mind, write them down, and analyze how they can be achieved. We will illustrate how to approach these goals practically, so that they may be fulfilled. First, we must emphasize that your goals should be specific. Second, they should be realistic. The following worksheet (Table 4) illustrates a typical

TABLE 4
Growth Strategy Feasibility Worksheet

GOAL	STRATEGY	POSSIBLE ACTIONS
To increase per unit sales by 10% annually for the next five years	Increase prices. Increase table turnover. Increase customer count. Diversify menu. Increase hours of operation. Improve price/value relationship.	Menu development. Increase promotion. Improve service techniques. Increase selections available. New recipes—Cook training.
To expand to five units in five years	Accumulate necessary financial resources.	Prepare pro forma financial statements. Estimate costs. Increase debt to banks. Increase equity from investors. Internal cash flow—operations.
	Location and concept development.	Management planning and/or outside services.
	Attract qualified management.	Promote from within company. Train new personnel.
	Staffing new operations.	Transfer present employees. Train new staff.
To diversify existing unit; open a lounge or discotheque	Analyze competition. Resource planning.	Prepare pro forma financial statements. Local government consent. Analyze present management capabilities. Hire an experienced manager. Train present management. Acquire required permits.

method of analyzing your goals and growth strategies. It gives detailed examples of your options and ways of accomplishing them.

The determination of whether a strategy is feasible varies from company to company as well as from unit to unit. A good start toward evaluating strategy is to determine if the necessary resources are available. Secondly, evaluate the project from a return on investment perspective.

THE FINANCIAL PLAN

Although investors and borrowers are interested in your concept and how well you personally sell the idea, most are primarily interested in just one thing—making money. Therefore, a solid financial statement is perhaps the most important factor to most financial backers. The prestige of being involved in a restaurant quickly loses its glamour if the operation is not profitable.

Lenders are most concerned that the restaurant will generate enough cash to comfortably service the debt. Therefore, interest coverages (earnings before taxes/interest) and principal payments are their primary concern.

Investors want to see what volume of sales and earnings can be expected from operations. They will also carefully scrutinize your financial statement to check for: 1) reasonable sales projections; 2) reasonable cost allowances; and 3) complete and logical handling of all financing matters. The following is a list of the statements that should be included in all business plans. This list should satisfy the lender and investor alike and supply sufficient information for both types of financial backers to make decisions on their interest in your venture.

1. Detailed Schedule of Estimated Start-up Costs
2. Pro forma Income Statements
   a. Monthly—the first 12 months
   b. Annually—the succeeding two years
3. Pro forma Cash Flow Statement—first 12 months

4. Pro forma Balance Sheet
5. Proposed Financing Schedule
6. Schedule of Return on Investment (ROI)
7. Schedule of Interest and Rental Coverages

An Example

The following pages demonstrate how the financial statement of a restaurant should be presented in a business plan. Our hypothetical restaurant (The Fish Fantasy) has the following characteristics:

Name: The Fish Fantasy
Type: Full Service
Menu: Limited
Fare: Seafood
Capacity: 175 Seats
Building: Leased
Cost/Sq. Ft.: 85¢/sq. ft. includes Common Area Maintenance (CAM) and taxes or 6% of gross sales, whichever is higher

Seasonality: Summer peak season
Location: Ridgewood, California
Sq. Ft.: 5,000 sq. ft.
Scheduled to Open: July 1, 1982

Estimated Annual
Volume:
Low: $ 660,000
Expected Case: $ 877,000
High: $1,000,000
Beverage: 25% of Total Sales
Food: 75% of Total Sales
Average Check (per person): Lunch: $3.80
Dinner: $5.50

Developing a Sales Forecast

A sales forecast is the basis on which the financial statements are developed. Sales projections require a number of assumptions, and care must be taken in their development to give a realistic scenario of future operations.

Two necessary assumptions needed to develop a sales forecast are:

1. Likely table turnover for lunch and dinner
2. Average check (per customer, sometimes called per-person expenditure or average cover)

Once these two items are estimated, the sales forecast can be developed as shown in Table 5.

Once sales have been forecast and the most likely scheme of things for the upcoming twelve months has been shown, further forecasting is possible. Three different pro forma income statements should be developed. A high, low, and most likely schedule of income should be presented. This gives investors and lenders a glimpse of the worst and best case possible as well as the most likely event. The expected case for the income statement is illustrated in Table 6. It is important to readers of these financial statements that all costs are presented as a percentage of sales. This gives readers an easy means of comparison to other restaurants in the industry. Table 6 is taken from the statements on pages 53-67.

As can be seen from Table 6, all costs other than food and beverage costs are computed as a percentage of *total sales*. Food and beverage costs are computed as a percent of respective sales.

Controllable Costs

You will need to develop the best estimates on all variable expenses expected. Use all available data such as competitors' costs, actual estimates from utility companies and suppliers, as well as industry figures to develop the most likely scenario for the new operation.

TABLE 5
Sales Forecast

	Low	Medium (Expected)	High
Lunch Sales	$231,000	$276,640	$ 350,000
Dinner Sales	429,000	600,600	650,000
Total Sales	$660,000	$877,240	$1,000,000

Sales Volume Projection—Expected Case

		Monday	Tuesday	Wednesday	Thursday	Friday	Saturday	Sunday
Average Weekly Lunch Sales	Expected Average Turnover	1.0	1.0	1.0	1.0	1.0	1.5	1.5
	Total Seating Capacity	175	175	175	175	175	175	175
	Expected Average Check per Customer	$3.80	$3.80	$3.80	$3.80	$3.80	$3.80	$3.80
	Total Sales	$665.00	$ 665.00	$ 665.00	$ 665.00	$ 665.00	$ 997.50	$ 997.50

		Monday	Tuesday	Wednesday	Thursday	Friday	Saturday	Sunday
Average Weekly Dinner Sales	Expected Average Turnover	1.0	1.25	1.25	1.5	2.5	2.5	2.0
	Total Seating Capacity	175	175	175	175	175	175	175
	Expected Average Check per Customer	$5.50	$5.50	$5.50	$5.50	$5.50	$5.50	$5.50
	Total Dinner Sales	$962.50	$1,203.13	$1,203.13	$1,443.75	$2,406.25	$2,406.25	$1,925.00

Total Expected Annual Sales: Lunch $276,640
Dinner 600,600
Total Sales $877,240 (To Income Statement)

TABLE 6

Income Statement (Expected)

SALES:

Food	$657,930	75%
Beverage	219,310	25
Total Sales	$877,240	100%

NOTES:

Food represents 75% of total sales

$$\text{Sales} \quad \frac{\$657,930}{\$877,240} = 0.75$$

Beverages represent 25% of total sales

$$\frac{\$219,310}{\$877,240} = 0.25$$

COST OF SALES:

Food	$276,331	42%
Beverage	61,407	28

When computing cost of sales percentages, compute both food cost and beverage cost as a percent of the related sales. Therefore, food cost and beverage cost as a percentage of sales are developed as follows:

$$\frac{\text{Food Costs}}{\text{Food Sales}} = \frac{\$276,331}{\$657,930} = 42\%$$

The same procedure is used for beverage costs.

A breakdown of the costs that should be given in supporting schedules for the items on the income statement is given in Table 7. Of course, some of these expenses may not be applicable to your particular restaurant and others may be added. This is just a general guideline, showing what types of items make up the figures on the income statement.

TABLE 6 (Cont'd)

TOTAL SALES:		$877,240	100.0%
Cost of Sales: Food	$276,331		
Beverage	61,407	337,738	38.5
Gross Profit:		$539,502	61.5%
CONTROLLABLE EXPENSES:			
Payroll		$193,000	22.0%
Employee Benefits		30,700	3.5
Advertising and Promotion		17,500	2.0
Total Other Expenses		209,798	23.9
TOTAL EXPENSES		$450,998	
INCOME BEFORE TAXES		$ 88,504	10.1%

Occupation Costs and Depreciation

These items include rental payments, common area maintenance charges, interest, and depreciation. An estimate of such costs
should be available for at least the upcoming twelve months. Figures for future years should reflect escalating costs and hence use a
rule-of-thumb figure for inflation of between five and ten percent.

Leases (Rentals) Minimum lease commitments should be ex-
plicitly stated in the contract. Leases based on a percentage of sales
can be developed by estimating sales for the period and deriving the
rental figure from the sales estimate.

Depreciation Utilize accelerated depreciation for tax purposes
and straight line depreciation for financial statement presentation.

TABLE 7

Controllable Expenses

ITEM	SUPPORTING SCHEDULE	
Payroll: $193,000	Service	$ 82,990
	Bartenders	9,650
	Preparation	52,110
	Sanitation	8,685
	General & Administrative	39,565
	Total Payroll	$193,000
Employee Benefits: $30,700	Payroll Taxes	$ 18,420
	Workers' Comp. Insurance	4,600
	Employee Benefits Insurance	7,050
	Misc. Employee Benefits	630
	Total Employee Benefits	$ 30,700
Direct Operating Expenses: $48,250	Laundry & Linen Rental	$ 8,100
	China & Glassware	5,300
	Silverware	2,000
	Kitchen Utensils	2,750
	Cleaning Supplies	5,500
	Paper Supplies	6,000
	Guest Supplies	10,800
	Service Bar Expense	2,000
	Menus & Wine Lists	1,800
	Contract Cleaning	4,000
	Total Operating Expenses	$ 48,250

Table 7 (Cont'd)

Advertising and Promotion: $17,500	Newspaper & Magazine	$ 15,000
	Advertising Agency Fees	2,500
	Total	$ 17,500
Utilities: $21,900	Electricity/gas	$ 15,000
	Water	5,150
	Waste Removal	1,750
	Total	$ 21,900
General and Administrative: $35,000	Office Supplies, Printing & Stationery	$ 2,500
	Telephone	1,750
	Dues & Subscriptions	1,750
	Insurance & General	18,000
	Credit Card Commission	10,000
	Protective & Bank Pickup	1,000
	Total	$ 35,000
Repairs and Maintenance: $2,600	Miscellaneous	$ 2,600
	TOTAL	$348,950

INDUSTRY SURVEY

The industry survey is an important, yet often overlooked portion of the business proposal. Basically the survey provides the reader with a good overview of the restaurant industry as a whole. Although you may know your operation very well, this section gives the reader an understanding of where the industry, in general, is headed.

This section should outline the trends, the recent history, and the overall characteristics of the restaurant industry. It should serve to enhance your plan while at the same time demonstrating your awareness of the major problems facing the industry. This will increase your credibility substantially.

CHAPTER THREE

THE SAMPLE PROPOSAL

INTRODUCTION

The first two chapters have outlined the necessary ingredients for the development of a high-quality, professional business plan. This chapter will present a complete business proposal which brings together all of these ingredients and presents a hypothetical restaurant, "The Fish Fantasy."

As stated earlier, many of the points presented in this business plan may be very similar to ones you will want to present in your own proposal. Other points may not apply to your situation. It is our intention to illustrate what a good business proposal should include, and not to dictate one particular presentation. Different situations require different proposals.

It should be remembered that a business proposal is both a planning tool and a selling instrument. It is a planning tool in that the development of such a proposal will force you to logically and carefully analyze and construct a successful restaurant by covering all of the important bases. Second, it is a selling instrument that will convey your intentions for the new venture in an attractive and sophisticated way to investors and lenders.

BUSINESS PROPOSAL
THE FISH FANTASY RESTAURANT
RIDGEWOOD, CALIFORNIA

NOTE: The following restaurant proposal was developed for illustrative purposes only. It is not intended to be used as a strict guideline, but as an example of how a proposal should be presented. All names, places, and financial data are completely fictitious. Your proposal may vary in content and order depending on your situation.

THE FISH FANTASY RESTAURANT
CONTENTS

1. SUMMARY

Fish Fantasy recognizes that dining is both a convenience and a form of entertainment. Our waiters and waitresses will greet the patrons with pleasant smiles and offer prompt, efficient service in our warm surroundings. High-quality food at reasonable prices will bring the customer back time and time again.

We will serve only choice, fresh seafood cooked to perfection on mesquite broilers. This produces an exquisite taste and all the nutrients of the seafood are retained. Fresh salads and homemade seafood soups will capture the diner's heart, please his palate, and bring a smile to his face—and all at reasonable prices.

The rapidly growing city of Ridgewood, California, will be the site of the first Fish Fantasy Restaurant. A top-notch management team of Frank Johnson and Mark Harris will put all this together in our 5,000-sq.-ft. location. The 175-seat restaurant will have a sales volume of $877,000 in its first year of operation and net approximately $88,000 before taxes. Our strategy is to carefully expand our high-quality, medium-priced restaurant concept to similar high-growth areas like Ridgewood to grow to 10 units with sales of $13 million within ten years.

A

2. THE MANAGEMENT TEAM

Frank Johnson, the president of the Fish Fantasy Restaurants, will be in charge of the marketing operations and finance. He is responsible for developing systems, advertising campaigns, growth strategies, policy-making, and control procedures. Frank has his B.S. from the University of California with emphasis in Marketing and Finance. He has worked in many restaurants as cook and manager. He was recently involved in the opening and training of personnel at the Fishing Pole Restaurant in Westwood Village. He is also involved in the California Small Business Consulting Service, developing a venture proposal for a client on a new fast food concept. Frank is a self-starting, hard-working individual. He is a creative marketer, involved in small businesses of his own since he was thirteen years old. The concept and recipes were developed by Frank while he was an undergraduate at University of California majoring in Marketing.

Mark Harris, vice president of operations and manager of the Fish Fantasy Restaurant, will be in charge of the restaurant's day-to-day operations. Specific duties include ordering, scheduling, training, and in-house advertising. Mark has worked for Steak 'n Such and The Sizzlin' Corral restaurants. He started with Far East Food Services after graduating from high school in 1970. He has worked for Western Restaurants, Inc. in the Bay Area and Seattle and is currently the store manager at their newest unit in Marina Woodside. Mark is very much a people-oriented person. His employees have a very close relationship with him and respect him as a manager.

The service manager will be someone with at least three to five years of full-service restaurant experience, either as a waiter or waitress. He/she should be young, energetic, and

B

love working with people. His/her duties will include recruiting, training, scheduling, and evaluation of all service personnel.

All management personnel must have the ability to grow and accept job expansion as the company grows. They must be highly motivated, career-oriented people.

C

3. CONCEPT

The Fish Fantasy Restaurant is a new concept in full-service fresh seafood restaurants. The restaurant will offer a limited selection of the freshest, most nutritiously prepared seafood available. Entrees will include broiled lobster, seafood Newburg, swordfish, and oysters on the half shell. There will also be a vast selection of fine seafood soups. The Fish Fantasy's wine list will be comprised of a wide selection of white wines from a California Chenin Blanc to a fine German Riesling.

The Fish Fantasy will have a casual nautical motif with aquariums, large hanging planters, and indoor waterfalls. Waiters and waitresses will be dressed in sailor attire.

The split-level dining area will have a seating capacity of 175. Diners will enjoy the atmosphere of hanging plants, used brick walkways, large picture windows, heavy wood tables, and open beam ceilings. A small waterfall and large saltwater fish aquariums will also add to the dining experience.

D

4. CUSTOMER PROFILE

The Fish Fantasy is designed to appeal to business and professional people seeking an informal atmosphere and quality dining at reasonable prices.

A significant portion of the dinner clientele will come from the surrounding area of Ridgewood. There are over 100,000 persons living within four square miles of the Fish Fantasy. The market will be segmented as illustrated in the following chart.

	CUSTOMER DESCRIPTION	POTENTIAL
Dinner Customers	Families and households	over 100,000 persons
Lunch Customers	Professional and business persons	over 500 firms in the area employing over 15,000 persons
	Students from the university	10,000 persons

A typical customer will be married, between the ages of twenty-two and forty-five, and have an average family income of $32,500 annually.

The following is demographic information compiled on the surrounding area.

E

POPULATION
COMMUNITIES IN THE CITY OF RIDGEWOOD

Community	Present	5/82	5/83
Appletree	30,000	34,500	39,675
Walnut Grove	6,400	7,360	8,464
Towngate	44,600	51,290	58,984
Northbridge	19,000	21,850	25,128
Total	100,000	115,000	132,251

Additional Demographic Information

The information below represents the resident profile in the City of Ridgewood as of January 15, 1981. Information supplied by the Chamber of Commerce.

Mean number of persons per household	2.8
Head of household is a college graduate	72%
Median family income	$32,500
Median age	36

F

5. LOCATION

The Fish Fantasy Restaurant will be located in the new Town Square Shopping Center, Ridgewood, California. The building will be free standing and built to suit by the developer. We have negotiated a ten-year lease with two five-year options on 5,000 square feet. The lease terms are $.85 per square foot, which includes taxes and common area maintenance or 6 percent of gross sales, whichever is greater.

The Fish Fantasy is the only restaurant of its type within five square miles. There will be other food service operations in Town Square which could be considered good generators of potential customers but not direct competition. It is our hope that the Town Square Center becomes known as a general place to go for both lunch and dinner.

G

6. COMPETITION

The food service industry happens to be one of the most competitive industries in the United States, California being even more so with over 45,000 permits issued, leading the nation in eating and drinking establishments. The Fish Fantasy will be entering a market containing nearly 100 food service establishments. These run the gamut from Burger Bash to Le Palace. The competitive advantages and disadvantages of the Fish Fantasy are assessed in the following chart.

Assessment of Competitive Advantages and Disadvantages

Name	Fish Fantasy	Johnny D's	Lobster Haven	Hawaiian Palace
Menu	Limited Seafood	Prime Rib	Seafood	Steak/ Seafood
Price	Medium	Medium	Medium	High
Hours	11 am- 11 pm	11 am- 12 am	5 pm- 12 am	5 pm- 12 am
Credit Cards Accepted	Master Card, Visa	None	Master Card, Visa	American Express, Master Card, Visa, Diners Club

H

As far as changes in competition in the future, the City Planning Department has informed us that there are no new shopping centers planned for the next three years, while the population of the area is projected to increase at over fifteen percent per year.

I

7. THE MARKETING PLAN

People

The Fish Fantasy Restaurant will cater its service to those persons who work and/or live in the city of Ridgewood. We feel, however, that once established, the reputation and quality of the Fish Fantasy will attract customers from other cities miles away.

Most of the employees, specifically cooks and service personnel, will be recruited from the university nearby. Contact has already been made with the director of job placement at Ridgewood College.

Product

As mentioned earlier, the Fish Fantasy will offer a fare of diverse fresh seafood selections. All items will be either baked, broiled, or barbecued in our mesquite barbecue pits. A copy of the menu and wine list appears in Appendix_____. (We did not supply the Appendix, but this illustrates how it can be used.)

Price

A limited selection of quality food will be the key to maintaining our medium price range. With limited choices, food costs can be more easily monitored and controlled. Excess product will be used in our delicious soup recipes.

All entrees will include a trip to the salad bar and fresh warm sourdough bread. The average check per person for

J

dinner will be in the $4.50-$6.00 range, exclusive of drinks. Lunch will range between $2.50 and $5.00.

Place

Again, the new Fish Fantasy Restaurant will be located in the Town Square Shopping Center, Ridgewood, California. We feel the area of Ridgewood offers the greatest possibility of success for a restaurant of this type due to the rapid growth and limited direct competition. Other restaurants located in the Town Square will generate a good number of potential customers, while none of them provide the quality fare and unique atmosphere of the Fish Fantasy.

Promotion and Advertising

The first year's promotion and advertising budget of $17,500 will be geared toward newspaper and magazine display ads. Most of the ads will be professionally developed and used with a "hook," such as a coupon or gift certificate, which will help determine the effectiveness of the ads.

K

8. ORGANIZATION AND PERSONNEL

Although inventory control is a key to profitability, people are the key to generating sales in a restaurant. With the exception of the full-time management, cooks, and bartenders, the Fish Fantasy will staff its operation with college men and women. These employees will be energetic, friendly, and intelligent. College students are mature enough to know when the patrons want to be left alone or when they wish more attention and service.

There will be no benefits for part-time employees. Full-time employees will be entitled to a two-week vacation after one year of service. The head line cook and prep cook will receive medical insurance in addition to paid vacation. Overtime will be paid to employees working over 40 hours per week at a rate of 1.5 times their hourly rate. Employee meals will be charged at one-half the menu price. Salads and soft drinks will not be charged.

The following chart illustrates the organizational structure of the Fish Fantasy Restaurant upon opening.

L

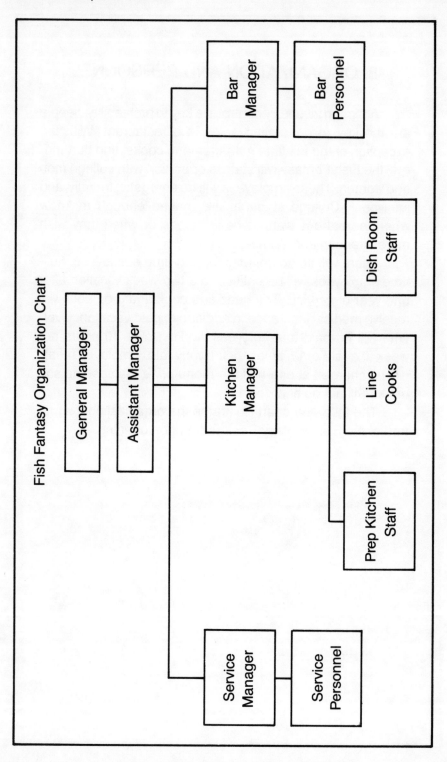

Fish Fantasy Organization Chart

9. OPERATIONS

The equipment for the Fish Fantasy Restaurant is being leased from California Restaurant Supply. They will draw up plans for plumbing, electricity, and gas as well as construct the kitchen and deliver the equipment. The schedule of costs appears in Schedule 1 on page 53.

The kitchen is being designed for the most efficient workflow. It consists of four work stations and a preparation (prep) area. The cooking line has been planned to require a minimum amount of reaching and walking at each station. Storage areas and small reach-ins located at each station reduce trips to the walk-in and storeroom during rush hours.

Food products and supplies are available through various food service distributors that service restaurants in the Ridgewood area. Mark Harris, vice president of operations for Fish Fantasy, has already developed good working relationships with many of these suppliers through his past experience with Western Restaurants, Inc. Fresh fish is available daily from Davey's Fresh Fish Locker at the Los Angeles harbor.

N

10. GROWTH STRATEGY

The Fish Fantasy Restaurant plans on opening its first restaurant on July 1, 1982. After three years of operation we plan to open our second restaurant in one of the following areas: North Park, San Viejo, Cartillo Beach, or Porgenville. These cities all indicate a high potential for a restaurant of our type. Table A below summarizes the planned growth in units and sales for the Fish Fantasy Restaurants.

TABLE A

Projected Growth of the Fish Fantasy Restaurants

Year	Number of Units	Projected Annual Revenues
1	1	$ 877,240
4	2	1,887,000
5	3	2,987,000
6	4	4,100,000
7	6	6,500,000
8	8	9,600,000
10	10	13,000,000

After five years the Fish Fantasy is also planning to establish a commissary to supply its restaurants with fresh seafood, baked goods, and canned food products.

O

11. THE FINANCIAL PLAN

The following schedules summarize the financing, projected revenues, and debt-service ability for the Fish Fantasy's first *four* years of operation. The schedules appear as follows:

Schedule 1 — Start-up Costs—Sources and Uses of Cash

Schedule 2 — Sales Forecast

Schedule 3 — Expense Schedule

Schedule 4 — Pro forma Income Statement (Year 1)

Schedule 5 — Cash Budget (Year 1)

Schedule 6 — Balance Sheet (End of Year 1)

Schedule 7 — Pro forma Income Statements (Years 2, 3, and 4)

Schedule 8 — Schedules of Return on Investment and Rental and Interest Coverages

Schedule 9 — Proposed Financing Schedule

P

SCHEDULE 1

Start-up Costs
Sources and Uses of Cash

SOURCES OF FUNDS
Equipment Financing	$112,500	
Equity Investment	430,700	
TOTAL SOURCES		$543,200

USES OF FUNDS
Lease Improvements	$300,000	
Kitchen Equipment	150,000	
Lease Deposits	10,200	
Supplies	10,000	
Food Inventory	8,000	
Beverage Inventory	6,000	
Liquor License	6,000	
Other Deposits	3,000	
TOTAL USES		$493,200

AVAILABLE WORKING CAPITAL TO
BEGIN OPERATION $ 50,000

Q

SCHEDULE 2 Sales Forecast

	(Expected)		
	Low	Medium	High
Lunch Sales	$231,000	$276,640	$ 350,000
Dinner Sales	429,000	600,600	650,000
Total Sales	$660,000	$877,240	$1,000,000

$ 5,320.00 Avg. Weekly Sales
52 No. of Weeks Open
$276,640.00 EXPECTED Annual Lunch/Dinner Sales

Sales Volume Projection—Expected Case

Average Weekly Lunch Sales	Monday	Tuesday	Wednesday	Thursday	Friday	Saturday	Sunday	Totals
Expected Average Turnover	1.0	1.0	1.0	1.0	1.0	1.5	1.5	8.0
Total Seating Capacity	175	175	175	175	175	175	175	175
Expected Average Check	$3.80	$3.80	$3.80	$3.80	$3.80	$3.80	$3.80	$3.80
Total Lunch Sales	$665.00	$ 665.00	$ 665.00	$ 665.00	$ 665.00	$ 997.50	$ 997.50	$ 5,320.00

Average Weekly Dinner Sales	Monday	Tuesday	Wednesday	Thursday	Friday	Saturday	Sunday	Totals
Expected Average Turnover	1.0	1.25	1.25	1.5	2.5	2.5	2.0	12.0
Total Seating Capacity	175	175	175	175	175	175	175	175
Expected Average Check	$5.50	$5.50	$5.50	$5.50	$5.50	$5.50	$5.50	$5.50
Total Dinner Sales	$962.50	$1,203.13	$1,203.12	$1,443.75	$2,406.25	$2,406.25	$1,925.00	$ 11,550.00

$ 11,550.00 Avg. Weekly Sales
52 No. of Weeks Open
$600,600.00 EXPECTED Annual Dinner Sales

Total Expected Annual Sales:
Lunch $276,640
Dinner 600,600
Total Sales $877,240

(TO INCOME STATEMENT)

SCHEDULE 3
Expense Schedule

	AMOUNT	% OF RESPECTIVE EXPENSES	% OF TOTAL SALES
PAYROLL			
Service	$ 82,990	43.0	
Bartenders	9,650	5.0	
Preparation	52,110	27.0	
Sanitation	8,685	4.5	
General & Administrative	39,565	20.5	
TOTAL PAYROLL	$193,000	100.0	22.0
EMPLOYEE BENEFITS			
Payroll Taxes	$ 18,420	60.0	
Workers' Comp. Ins.	4,600	15.0	
Employee Benefits Ins.	7,050	23.0	
Other Employee Benefits	630	2.0	
TOTAL EMPLOYEE BENEFITS	$ 30,700	100.0	3.5
ADVERTISING & PROMOTION			
Newspaper & Magazine	$ 15,000	86.0	
Advertising Agency Fees	2,500	14.0	
Billboards	—	—	
Radio & Television	—	—	
TOTAL ADVERTISING & PROMOTION	$ 17,500	100.0	2.0

S

SCHEDULE 3 (Cont'd)

	AMOUNT	% OF RESPECTIVE EXPENSES	% OF TOTAL SALES
DIRECT OPERATING EXPENSES			
Laundry & Linen Rental	$ 8,100	16.8	
China & Glassware	5,300	11.0	
Silverware	2,000	4.1	
Kitchen Utensils	2,750	5.7	
Cleaning Supplies	5,500	11.4	
Paper Supplies	6,000	12.4	
Guest Supplies	10,800	22.4	
Service Bar Expense	2,000	4.1	
Menus & Wine Lists	1,800	3.7	
Contract Cleaning	4,000	8.4	
TOTAL DIRECT OPERATING EXPENSES	$48,250	100.0	5.5

T

SCHEDULE 3 (Cont'd)

	AMOUNT	% OF RESPECTIVE EXPENSES	% OF TOTAL SALES
UTILITIES			
Gas & Electricity	$15,000	68.0	
Water	5,150	24.0	
Waste Removal	1,750	8.0	
TOTAL UTILITIES	$21,900	100.0	2.5
GENERAL & ADMINISTRATIVE EXPENSES			
Office Supplies, Printing, Stationery	$ 2,500	7.0	
Telephone	1,750	5.0	
Dues & Subscriptions	1,750	5.0	
Insurance—General	18,000	51.0	
Credit Card Commissions	10,000	29.0	
Protective & Bank Pickup	1,000	3.0	
TOTAL GENERAL & ADMINISTRATIVE	$35,000	100.0	4.0
REPAIRS & MAINTENANCE	$ 2,600	100.0	0.3

U

SCHEDULE 4
Pro Forma Income Statement
Monthly for the Year Ending
June 30, 1983

	YEAR ENDING JUNE 30, 1983		JUL
SALES:			
Food	$657,930	75.0%	$60,310
Beverage	219,310	25.0	20,103
TOTAL SALES	$877,240	100.0%	$80,413
COST OF SALES:			
Food	$276,331	42.0%	$25,330
Beverage	61,407	28.0	5,629
Total Cost of Sales	337,738	38.5%	30,959
GROSS PROFIT	$539,502	61.5%	$49,454
CONTROLLABLE EXPENSES:			
Payroll	$193,000	22.0%	$17,692
Employee Benefits	30,700	3.5	2,814
Advertising & Promotion	17,500	2.0	1,604
Direct Operating	48,250	5.5	4,423
Utilities	21,900	2.5	2,008
General & Administrative	35,000	4.0	3,208
Repairs & Maintenance	2,600	0.3	238
TOTAL CONTROLLABLE EXPENSES	$348,950	39.8%	$31,987
OCCUPATION COSTS, DEPRECIATION & INTEREST:			
Rental Expense	$ 52,635	6.0%	$ 4,825
Depreciation—Furniture, Fixtures & Equipment	39,286	4.4	3,274
Interest	10,127	1.2	934
TOTAL OCCUPATION COSTS	$102,048	11.6%	$ 9,033
TOTAL EXPENSES	$450,998	51.5%	$41,020
INCOME BEFORE TAXES	$ 88,504	10.1%	$ 8,434

V

SCHEDULE 4 (Cont'd)
Pro Forma Income Statement
Monthly for the Year Ending
June 30, 1983

AUG	SEPT	OCT	NOV
$60,310	$60,310	$49,345	$49,345
20,103	20,103	16,448	16,448
$80,413	$80,413	$65,793	$65,793
$25,330	$25,330	$20,725	$20,725
5,629	5,629	4,605	4,605
30,959	30,959	25,330	25,330
$49,454	$49,454	$40,463	$40,463
$17,692	$17,692	$14,475	$14,475
2,814	2,814	2,303	2,303
1,604	1,604	1,313	1,313
4,423	4,423	3,619	3,619
2,008	2,008	1,642	1,642
3,208	3,208	2,625	2,625
238	238	195	195
$31,987	$31,987	$26,172	$26,172
$ 4,825	$ 4,825	$ 3,947	$ 3,947
3,274	3,274	3,274	3,274
918	902	886	869
$ 9,017	$ 9,001	$ 8,107	$ 8,090
$41,004	$40,988	$34,279	$34,262
$ 8,450	$ 8,466	$ 6,184	$ 6,201

W

SCHEDULE 4 (Cont'd)
Pro Forma Income Statement
Monthly for the Year Ending
June 30, 1983

	DEC	JAN	FEB
SALES:			
Food	$49,345	$49,345	$49,345
Beverage	16,448	16,448	16,448
TOTAL SALES	$65,793	$65,793	$65,793
COST OF SALES:			
Food	$20,725	$20,725	$20,725
Beverage	4,605	4,605	4,605
Total Cost of Sales	25,330	25,330	25,330
GROSS PROFIT	$40,463	$40,463	$40,463
CONTROLLABLE EXPENSES:			
Payroll	$14,475	$14,475	$14,475
Employee Benefits	2,303	2,303	2,303
Advertising & Promotion	1,313	1,313	1,313
Direct Operating	3,619	3,619	3,619
Utilities	1,642	1,642	1,642
General & Administrative	2,625	2,625	2,625
Repairs & Maintenance	195	195	195
TOTAL CONTROLLABLE EXPENSES	$26,172	$26,172	$26,172
OCCUPATION COSTS, DEPRECIATION & INTEREST:			
Rental Expense	$ 3,947	$ 3,947	$ 3,947
Depreciation—Furniture, Fixtures & Equipment	3,274	3,274	3,274
Interest	853	836	820
TOTAL OCCUPATION COSTS	$ 8,074	$ 8,057	$ 8,041
TOTAL EXPENSES	$34,246	$34,229	$34,213
INCOME BEFORE TAXES	$ 6,217	$ 6,234	$ 6,250

X

SCHEDULE 4 (Cont'd)
Pro Forma Income Statement
Monthly for the Year Ending
June 30, 1983

MAR	APR	MAY	Seasonal Index JUN
$49,345	$60,310	$60,310	$60,310
16,448	20,103	20,103	20,107
$65,793	$80,413	$80,413	$80,417
$20,725	$25,330	$25,330	$25,331
4,605	5,629	5,629	5,632
25,330	30,959	30,959	30,963
$40,463	$49,454	$49,454	$49,454
$14,475	$17,692	$17,692	$17,690
2,303	2,814	2,814	2,812
1,313	1,604	1,604	1,602
3,619	4,423	4,423	4,421
1,642	2,008	2,008	2,008
2,625	3,208	3,208	3,210
195	238	238	240
$26,172	$31,987	$31,987	$31,983
$ 3,947	$ 4,825	$ 4,825	$ 4,828
3,274	3,274	3,274	3,272
803	786	769	751
$ 8,024	$ 8,885	$ 8,868	$ 8,851
$34,196	$40,872	$40,855	$40,834
$ 6,267	$ 8,582	$ 8,599	$ 8,620

Y

SCHEDULE 5
Pro Forma Pretax Cash Budget
Monthly for Year Ended June 30, 1983

1982	JULY	AUGUST	SEPTEMBER	OCTOBER	NOVEMBER	DECEMBER
SOURCES OF CASH:						
Pretax Profits	$ 8,434	$ 8,450	$ 8,466	$ 6,184	$ 6,201	$ 6,217
Depreciation	3,274	3,274	3,274	3,274	3,274	3,274
Principal Payments on Note	(931)	(947)	(963)	(979)	(1,001)	(1,012)
NET CASH FLOW	$ 10,777	$ 10,777	$ 10,777	$ 8,479	$ 8,474	$ 8,479
BEGINNING CASH BALANCE	50,000	60,777	71,554	82,331	90,810	99,284
ENDING CASH BALANCE	$ 60,777	$ 71,554	$ 82,331	$ 90,810	$ 99,284	$107,763

1983	JANUARY	FEBRUARY	MARCH	APRIL	MAY	JUNE
SOURCES OF CASH:						
Pretax Profits	$ 6,234	$ 6,250	$ 6,267	$ 8,582	$ 8,599	$ 8,620
Depreciation	3,274	3,274	3,274	3,274	3,274	3,274
Principal Payments on Note	(1,029)	(1,045)	(1,062)	(1,079)	(1,096)	(1,116)
NET CASH FLOW	$ 8,479	$ 8,479	$ 8,479	$ 10,777	$ 10,777	$ 10,778
BEGINNING CASH BALANCE	107,763	116,242	124,721	133,200	143,977	154,754
ENDING CASH BALANCE	$116,242	$124,721	$133,200	$143,977	$154,754	$165,532

SCHEDULE 6
Fish Fantasy Restaurant—Pro Forma Balance Sheet
June 30, 1983

ASSETS:

Cash	$165,532
Food & Beverage Inventory	14,000
Supplies	10,000
Miscellaneous Deposits	13,200
Liquor License, at cost	6,000
Kitchen Equipment & Leasehold	
Improvements	450,000
Less Accumulated Depreciation	(39,286)
TOTAL ASSETS	$619,446

LIABILITIES:

Note Payable (Equipment)	$100,242

STOCKHOLDERS' EQUITY

Common Stock	$430,700
Retained Earnings*	88,504

TOTAL LIABILITIES AND	
STOCKHOLDERS' EQUITY	$619,446

Author's Note: Retained earnings should be net income after appropriate federal and state income taxes. No taxes were used in this illustration.

AA

SCHEDULE 7
Pro Forma
Income Statement

Years Ending June 30, 1984, 85, 86
Assuming 12% Annual Compounded Growth in Sales
For Initial Unit

	1984		1985		1986	
	AMOUNT	%	AMOUNT	%	AMOUNT	%
SALES:						
Food	$736,882	75.0%	$ 825,307	75.0%	$ 924,344	75.0%
Beverage	245,627	25.0	275,102	25.0	308,115	25.0
TOTAL SALES	$982,509	100.0%	$1,100,409	100.0%	$1,232,459	100.0%
COST OF SALES:						
Food	$309,490	42.0%	$ 346,630	42.0%	$ 388,225	42.0%
Beverage	68,775	28.0	77,092	28.0	86,272	28.0
Total Cost of Sales	378,265	38.5	423,722	38.5	474,497	38.5
GROSS PROFIT:	$604,244	61.5%	$ 676,687	61.5%	$ 757,962	61.5%

SCHEDULE 7 (Cont'd)

CONTROLLABLE EXPENSES:						
Payroll	$216,160	22.0%	$242,099	22.0%	$271,150	22.0%
Empoyee Benefits	34,384	3.5	38,510	3.5	43,131	3.5
Advertising & Promotion	19,600	2.0	21,952	2.0	24,586	2.0
Direct Operating	54,040	5.5	60,525	5.5	67,788	5.5
Utilities	24,528	2.5	27,471	2.5	30,768	2.5
General & Administrative	39,200	4.0	43,904	4.0	49,172	4.0
Repairs & Maintenance	7,860	0.8	13,205	1.2	19,720	1.6
TOTAL CONTROLLABLE EXPENSES:	$395,772	40.3%	$447,666	40.7%	$506,315	41.1%
OCCUPATION COSTS, DEPRECIATION, INTEREST:						
Rental Expense	$58,950	6.0%	$66,025	6.0%	$73,947	6.0%
Depreciation—Furniture, Fixtures, Equipment	39,286	4.0	39,286	3.6	39,286	3.2
Interest Expense	10,064	1.0	8,759	0.8	7,325	0.6
TOTAL OCCUPATION EXPENSES	$108,300	11.0%	$114,070	10.4%	$120,558	9.8%
TOTAL EXPENSES	$504,072	51.3%	$561,736	51.1%	$626,873	50.9%
INCOME BEFORE TAXES	$100,172	10.2%	$114,951	10.4%	$131,089	10.6%

SCHEDULE 8
Schedules of Rental & Interest Coverages, Return on Equity, Sales, Assets

YEARS ENDING JUNE 30

	1983	1984	1985	1986
Earnings Before Taxes	$ 88,504	$100,172	$115,014	$131,089
Rentals	52,635	58,950	66,025	73,947
Interest	10,127	10,064	8,759	7,325
Depreciation	39,286	39,286	39,286	39,286
Totals	$190,552	$208,472	$229,084	$251,647
(Rentals & Interest) Coverage*	3.04X	3.02X	3.06X	3.10X
PRETAX				
Return on Sales	10.0%	10.2%	10.4%	10.6%
Return on Assets	16.3	16.2	17.2	19.6
Return on Equity	20.5	19.3	18.6	17.9

*Represents earnings before taxes, rentals, interest, and depreciation divided by the sum of interest and rental expense. This is a measure of ability to cover rentals and interest payments.

DD

SCHEDULE 9
Fish Fantasy Restaurant
Proposed Financing Schedule

NAME	# OF SHARES	% OWNER- SHIP	CASH INVESTMENT
Frank Johnson	15,000	15%	$ 64,605
Mark Harris	15,000	15	64,605
Nathaniel Snyder, D.D.S.	20,000	20	86,140
J. Roland Simpson	20,000	20	86,140
Carolyn T. Williger	15,000	15	64,605
Restaurant Venture Capital Group	15,000	15	64,605
	100,000	100%	$430,700

EE

12. INDUSTRY SURVEY

The industry survey need not be long and elaborate, nor need it be difficult to research. Key topics that should be covered include the estimated growth in the industry and more specifically in the particular market segment your restaurant will fall into. This macro view gives the reader a general picture of the state of the industry and its potential.

Specific topics that should be highlighted include the trend in the price-value relationship between food away from home and food at home. With more families having two members in the work force, a larger percentage of meals are being eaten away from home. The broad spectrum of choices and the convenience factor combine to create a given value perception by the customer. The relative price level of food purchased and prepared at home is a major factor affecting this value perception.

Although at the current time there are no future government mandated minimum wage increases, this has been a major concern of restaurateurs over the past four years. The impact of potential increases should be evaluated.

Other trends that you identify should be detailed and explained vis à vis their possible favorable or unfavorable impact on your proposed operation.

FF

APPENDIX

The appendix should contain supplemental information such as résumés and personal balance sheets of the key personnel, and any developmental work that has already been completed, such as copies of menus, renderings, or kitchen layouts. The further along you are in these types of processes, the more credibility you will have with potential investors and lenders. The more you have done to date and the more money you have committed, are factors which will create confidence and commitment in the minds of others.

GG

CHAPTER FOUR

OTHER TOPICS OF IMPORTANCE

ACCOUNTING SYSTEMS

Business records and control systems provide a foundation for a successful operation and a valuable tool for obtaining future loans and achieving long-term growth plans. With the advice of an accountant, the restaurateur can create a tailor-made system to satisfy the specific needs of his business. There are prepackaged systems available through stationers designed for use in restaurants and bars. A few of the systems available are listed below:

- *The Ideal System: Bookkeeping and Tax Records for Restaurants and Cafés.* Stock No. 3221.
  This is available through the Ideal System Company, P.O. Box 1030, Berkeley, CA 94701. Contains income and expense records as well as accounts receivable, accounts payable, and cash. Specifically designed for restaurant operations.

- *Uniform System of Accounts for Restaurants.*
  Available through the National Restaurant Association,

311 First St., NW, Washington, D.C. 20001. It is a manual containing a system for classification of restaurants with a detailed explanation of accounts and procedures.

- *Simplex Bookkeeping and Income Tax Record for Restaurants.* Item No. 34203.
  Dennison National, Holyoke, MA 01041. Contains forms for two years, business including: daily transaction records, employees' earnings records, instruction and demonstration entries. Available through local office supply stores.

- *Simplified Master System for Restaurants.*
  Available through Simplified Business Service, Inc., 901 Barclay Bldg., Canyonwood, PA 19004. Very complete system is also available through local distributors.

ADVERTISING

The restaurateur may be a total professional when it comes to his/her concept, competition, and customer, but he/she can be a complete amateur when it comes to advertising. The major inadequacies usually found in a restaurant advertising plan include:

1. *Lack of Planning.* Advertising should be seventy-five percent planning and 25 percent implementation. The restaurateur is usually so caught up in the day-to-day operations that little time is given to planning and the program is usually spotty and inconsistent.

2. *Patchy Advertising.* Due to lack of planning the restaurateur often ends up with an inconsistent and unexciting program. He/she wastes time and money on the wrong type of media for reaching the target market.

3. *Lack of Cost Effectiveness.* It usually does not pay for the small restaurant owner to put money into radio, television, or major newspapers. Neighborhood newspapers serve as good advertising

media. Many independents have great success with direct mail campaigns targeted to the immediate neighborhood with some type of coupon or other tangible way to determine the effectiveness of the campaign.

Transit advertising is often overlooked. You can buy a poster on the back of a bus (bus tail) for a reasonable amount.

4. *Attempts to Do Too Much with a Single Ad.* Many times someone with a small business tries to do too much with a single ad and the message is lost. You should concentrate on a single entrée, a happy hour, or a special Sunday brunch, but not all of these.

5. *Little Understanding of Ad Agencies and Campaign Strategy.* Most independents feel that they cannot afford an agency, or they rely on media that often defeat the purpose of the campaign. In most cities there is a tremendous amount of free-lance talent as well as one- and two-person agencies. For surprisingly little per month, the restaurateur can have an effective program in the community. These people are professionals and can help you develop a feel, a theme, a consistent look, so that the advertising becomes identified with your restaurant.

It is much more desirable to do many smaller, consistent ads all year long than to spend the whole year's budget on one large advertisement.

BUYING AN EXISTING BUSINESS

An alternative to starting a new restaurant is buying an existing business. You may discover very profitable operations as well as turnaround situations. An advantage of buying an existing business is that many times you can purchase it with less capital. Because of what is known as an installment sale, it is very common for an owner to require only a small amount of cash down and to take a note on the balance.

If you prefer to buy an existing business in order to completely change the concept and decor, a word of warning: it is not as simple as it appears. It is difficult to change the image in the eyes of the community, particularly if the image was negative. Another problem frequently encountered is old and poorly maintained equipment.

One advantage of buying an existing business is that you frequently will be operating at a profit. The day after purchase, you have an established clientele and have eliminated most of the difficult and expensive chores encountered with opening a new business. The following outline covers the basics that you should know before purchasing an existing restaurant. To locate opportunities, check listings in major papers under business opportunities, restaurant trade journals, or contact a Business Opportunities Broker. There are some brokers that specialize in food service operations.

Back-Up Monies

These are monies that are needed to purchase a business over and above the full price on a cash deal or above the down payment on an installment sale. Listed on the opposite page are examples of items for which back-up monies should be appropriated in a new operation.

Bulk Sales Escrow

Section 6-102 of the Uniform Commercial Code protects the buyer and the creditors. It also allows that:

- All equipment must be in good working order at the time physical possession is granted to the buyer.
- Before the seller gets all of his/her monies from escrow, he/she must get releases from the State Board of Equalization (for sales tax) and the Department of Benefit Payments (for employees).
- If the ABC is involved, the investigating officer will want to see a copy of the lease and lease assignment.
- The Office of the County Recorder must be notified at

Back-up Monies Needed in the Purchase
of an Existing Restaurant Operation*

Purpose	Approx. Amount	Returnable
Lease deposit—first and last month's rent	$2 \times$ (1 month's rent)	1 month's rent
Utility deposit	$200-$250	$200-$250
Inventory	$4,000-$20,000	$4,000-$20,000
Sales tax on fixture valuation	$5,000 \times 0.06 = $300	$500 tax credit
Insurance bond with the Board of Equalization	$100	-0-
Insurance (Liability)	$200	-0-
Escrow fees	varies	-0-
Proration of personal property taxes	$12-$50 month	-0-
Licenses, health permits	$100-$600	-0-
Cash on hand	$10,000-$100,000	$10,000-$100,000

*The figures in this example may vary depending on the size and location of the operation.

> least ten days before the sale is consummated.
> - A notice of intent to sell must be published in a general circulation newspaper in the judicial district in which the property is being sold.
> - A notice to the County Tax Collector of the county or counties involved must be personally delivered or sent by registered mail ten days before sale.

Alcoholic Beverage Control Laws

To transfer a liquor license, the investigator will want to review the following points with you:

- Where you have been employed for the past five years.
- If you have ever been arrested or had a fine in excess of fifty dollars.
- Where the money came from to purchase the business.
- Fingerprints of all parties whose names will appear on the license must be taken.
- If a buyer is married he/she may go on the license without the spouse's name; however, if the spouse is going to work even part-time in the business, his/her name must also appear on the license.
- All monies must be in escrow before a license can be transferred.
- The transfer takes thirty-five to forty-five days.

Again, laws vary from state to state.

Items to Check in Valuing a Restaurant

Fixture Valuation—twenty to seventy percent of selling price.
Taxable Fixtures—You must pay sales tax on this value. These fixtures are those that are used for holding or storing taxable merchandise, such as display ice boxes holding beer, wine, soda, etc.
Nontaxable Fixtures—These are fixtures that sales tax is not applied to. These fixtures are used to hold nontaxable items, basically grocery items.

These items would not be a factor if the business sale involves a purchase of a corporation.

Investment Tax Credit (Maximum ten percent)

Property must be depreciable and have a useful life of at least three years. The credit can be carried back three years and then forward for seven succeeding years. Check with your accountant concerning the percentage applicable to your situation.

Items of Major Importance Sometimes Overlooked

Leases
1. Is the lease assignable?
2. Percentage lease? What percentage?
3. CAM? If the lease is triple net, the lessor may have to pay the property tax and a common area maintenance fees.
4. Options? Renewal option?
5. Years remaining?
6. Cost-of-living increases?

Books and Records
1. Were the owners skimming?
2. Were they padding business expenses with personal expenses?
3. Number of days and hours. Will you be able to significantly increase volume/profitability through being open an extra day or increased hours of operation?

Contracts
1. Are there any? (Vending machines)
2. Vendors can sometimes be a good source of funds. They may deduct payments from your share of the vending revenues.

BUYING A FRANCHISE

Franchises are playing an increasingly important role in the food service industry with a high concentration in the fast-food segment. There are over 300 known fast-food franchisors with over 6,000 units competing in the marketplace.

Franchising offers many advantages to a new restaurateur. Affiliation with a reputable franchise operation often increases the availability of financing. Further advantages and disadvantages of franchises are outlined in Table 8.

TABLE 8
Advantages and Disadvantages of Franchising

ADVANTAGES	DISADVANTAGES
• Availability of financing	• Franchise fee
• Proven concept	• Royalty fee based on sales
• Training program	• Advertising assessments
• National advertising	• Fixed plan, little room for
• Usually lower initial cash requirements	creativity
• Help in site selection	
• Licensed use of trademark	
• Territorial rights	
• Exclusively developed equipment	

If you are considering a franchise, you should proceed with caution. There are many good and bad franchises. The Bank of America prints a check list of fifty questions that should be asked before contracting with a franchisor. This list can be obtained by sending a stamped, self-addressed envelope to: Bank of America, P.O. Box 37000, San Francisco, CA 94137. Further sources of franchising information are listed below:

Director of Franchising Organizations
Pilot Books
347 Fifth Avenue
New York, NY 10016

The Franchise Annual
National Franchise Reports
333 North Michigan Avenue
Chicago, IL 60601

Franchise Opportunities Handbook
U.S. Department of Commerce
Washington, D.C. 20230

Bank of America
Small Business Reporter
Franchising Vol. 9, No. 9, 1975
Department 3120
P.O. Box 37000
San Francisco, CA 94137

Small Business Administration
Expanding Sales Through Franchising
Management Aid #182
S.B.A., Washington, D.C. 20416
GPO-878-152

1978 Franchise Annual
(Lists 1,200 franchised headquarters with descriptions of business plus total investments. Sample contract and a How-To Handbook.) $14.95 plus $2.00 first class postage.
Info Press
736 Center Street
Lewiston, NY 14092

Robert Metz, *Franchising: How to Select a Business of Your Own*
New York, Hawthorn Books, Inc., 1969.
$10.00
Metz points out keys to successful franchising.

EQUIPMENT: BUY OR LEASE

There are as many different suppliers as there are ways to acquire equipment. A few decisions which must be made include: Which equipment company to use? Buy or lease? New or used?

It is our recommendation that you choose a reputable company that offers many services, has access to many manufacturers, and can offer a full line of equipment. These companies can offer you suggestions on quality, maintenance, capacity, etc., according to your particular concept and menu.

Although utilizing a full-service equipment company will be more expensive at the outset, we feel that this can save that much more in the long run through reduced labor cost, maintenance and repair costs, replacement costs, and reduced utility bills.

The buy or lease decision is an important one that should not be hastily made. And it does not have to be just one or the other; it can be a combination of the two. You may want to buy all your kitchen equipment and lease your electronic cash register. Another option would be to sell the entire package (land, building, and equipment) to an investor and lease the whole package back. This sale-leaseback arrangement could also be done through a financial institution.

The real decision to buy or lease will come down to an accounting and tax decision. There will be differences in cash flow and tax liability, which should be discussed with your accountant. The decision can have a significant effect on a firm's balance sheet.

FACILITIES: DESIGN AND LAYOUT

Another key element for the success of a food service operation is the design and layout of the facilities. This section is not designed to make the food service operator an expert in the field of design, but rather to familiarize him or her with the principles involved so that he or she can ask the right questions and convey the right information to the designers and architects.

When using the word "design" we are referring to the size, style, shape, and decor of the operation. "Layout" refers to the arrangement of the furnishings and equipment within the operation.

There are a few basic objectives that should be kept in mind when designing food service facilities.

- Design for efficient traffic flow, delivery, and pick-up.
- Provide working conditions conducive to productivity.
- Minimize the distance between preparation and service areas.
- Arrange compact work stations to minimize employee movement at the stations and in the service and kitchen areas.
- All operations should be on the same floor level.
- Plan a continuous flow of materials. Storage facilities and delivery docks should be arranged to provide a continuous flow of materials without backtracking.

For those persons new to this area, it is recommended that you consult competent advisors before attempting the design on your own operation. A *Buyer's Guide* available through most state restaurant associations can be used to locate consultants and designers in your area.

There are many firms that now offer the restaurateur a complete turnkey package. Such firms may offer the following services:

- feasibility study
- site location
- design
- layout
- construction
- equipment
- utensil supply
- food products supply

These companies have a wide range of talents and services and many times work on a cost-plus basis. They can be a great asset should you decide to franchise your concept by offering your franchisee a turnkey operation with relatively little work on your part.

Table 9 supplies rules of thumb for determining the size of an operation based on the type of operation and number of seats.

TABLE 9

Rule of Thumb for Determining Operation Size*

Type of Service	Kitchen Area Sq. Ft. per Dining Seat	Back of the House Area Sq. Ft. per Dining Seat	Dining Room Area Sq. Ft. per Dining Seat	Turnover in Patrons per Seat per Hour (at peak hours)
Cafeteria Commercial	6-8	10-12	13-18	1.5-2.5
Lunch Rooms Coffee Shop	4-6	8-10	18-26	1.0-2.5
Table Service with Dining Room	5-7	10-12	13-18	0.3-1.0

*These figures can vary depending on shape of dining room and quality of service.

FINANCING

Debt Financing

Generally, banks and other lenders are wary of lending money to start-up situations, particularly restaurant start-ups. However, by knowing what these lenders look for in a potential borrower, you can significantly increase your chances for successfully securing the funds needed to begin operation. If you can meet certain general qualifications, there are many avenues open to obtain financing.

The following is a general outline of qualifications that a borrower must meet for almost every type of financing.

1. Roughly twenty percent or more of start-up costs must be contributed by the equity investors to the business.
2. Related business experience—a successful track record is a decided advantage.
3. Strong personal credit.
4. Ability to repay the loan.
5. A sound concept and business plan.
6. Industry potential.

Of course, many of these qualifications have varying degrees of importance according to the particulars of the situation and the individuals involved.

The most important qualification to help you obtain credit is a strong personal financial statement. Lenders feel more at ease when they know that if the business should fail, they can fall back on your collateral to collect the debt.

Most of the necessary data for a bank to make a judgment on a loan request will be found in a completed business plan. This plan can be taken to all types of borrowers.

Table 10 describes the sources and types of loans available to restaurant operations.

TABLE 10
Debt Financing

SOURCE	TYPE OF LOAN	COMMENTS
Bank	Unsecured Term Equipment Equipment Leasing Real Estate Working Capital	Most widely used source of funds. Also good for future growth needs.
Commercial Finance Company	Equipment Real Estate Equipment Leasing Working Capital	Generally *higher interest* rates than banks. Should be second avenue of borrowing.
Insurance Company	Policy Loan Real Estate	Most conservative lenders. Need good credit or highly valued real estate as collateral.
Small Business Administration	Term Loan, Guaranteed Line of Credit	Special preferences for minority and handicapped. Six months to one year to process loans.
Savings & Loan Company	Real Estate	Generally require compensating balance.
Loan Development Company	Miscellaneous	State administered programs, similar to SBA. Primarily used to assist minority and handicapped.

Equity Financing

This is probably the best means of financing a start-up operation. Favorable aspects of this financing vehicle include: less risk for the entrepreneur, fewer restrictions, no absentee management, no interest or dividend payments expected, numerous ways to put together a deal, as well as improved financial condition in which to borrow for short-term financing or real-estate financing. Less favorable aspects of equity financing include reduced ownership and increased reporting to stockholders.

Most equity investors regard the individual entrepreneur's track record as the most influential ingredient in their decision to finance the start-up. Also important is a well-developed business plan with detailed financial statements. Some investors may desire a means of withdrawing their capital in a few years. This aspect is negotiable.

Table 11 lists the services and types of equity capital available.

INSURANCE

Knowing what type of insurance and how much to carry is an important aspect of good management. In the restaurant business, it is possible to lose the benefits of many years of hard work due to a single theft, fire, or accident.

Insurance planning can help avoid these devastating results. Good planning begins with the consideration of all the risks faced by the enterprise and then determining which can be covered by insurance. An insurance agent should be consulted to aid you in developing a comprehensive insurance package. The agent can also help work out employee benefit and insurance programs. Below is a list of the many types of insurance available.

- *Workers' Compensation* is required by law in most states and protects employees injured on the job against loss of wages and medical expenses.
- *Product Liability* insurance protects the restaurateur

TABLE 11

Equity Financing

SOURCE	TYPE OF ISSUE	COMMENTS
Nonprofessional Investor	Partnership Stock Issue Convertible Debt Options	Best means of financing start-ups. Terms very negotiable. Favorable tax implications for investors. Absentee ownership. Few restrictions.
Venture Capitalists (Small Business Investment Companies, SBIC)	Stock Ownership Convertible Debt	Usually venture capitalists influence management decisions. Have restrictions and limitations similar to banks. Usually desire part ownership in order to participate in equity build up.

against law suits due to food and beverages served.

- *Business Interruption* insurance allows the restaurant owner to recapture money lost when the restaurant is closed due to certain disasters.
- *Crime Coverage* insures against theft of cash by thieves or employees.
- *Fire and Property Damage* covers damage to equipment and fixtures caused by fire, wind, or explosion.
- *Personal Injury* protects against claims of libel, slander, or false arrest.
- *Glass Insurance* protects against damage to windows and mirrors.
- *Fidelity Bonds* protect against embezzlement by employees with access to business funds.
- *Dram Shop* insurance protects restaurants that serve cocktails against injuries to patrons or others outside the restaurant caused by an intoxicated customer.
- *Key Man* insurance protects the firm against business losses caused by the death or disability of key management personnel.
- *Special Multiperil Program (SMP)*. This is a recent addition to the insurance industry. The SMP program allows the restaurateur to cover all the risks previously mentioned except Workers' Compensation and company-owned automobiles. Combining most of the coverages into one package drastically reduces the policy writing and handling costs and therefore results in reduced premiums.

INVENTORY CONTROL

The periodic physical inventory is the most common method of evaluation, usually taken at the end of each week or month. Physical inventory refers to the actual physical counting of food quantities in inventory. These quantities are then multiplied by their unit costs in order to arrive at a total dollar value. The food cost is then determined in the manner shown in Table 12.

TABLE 12

Computation of Food Cost

Beginning Inventory	$ 4,000
Additional Purchases	12,000
Less: Ending Inventory	(5,000)
COST OF FOOD SOLD	$11,000

Inventories are usually valued at cost due to their relatively small size and rapid turnover. The same procedure should be used to inventory liquor and supplies. Inventory usage figures become a valuable management tool through trend analysis and comparison to industry averages. Once costs are presented as a percent of sales these can be compared to those of prior months to detect rising costs, and can be compared with the industry to uncover areas of concern. An out-of-line food cost may be the result of poor pricing, over-portioning, pilferage, or spoilage. These problems can be quickly detected and corrected before they become serious.

JOB DESCRIPTIONS

Job descriptions are detailed lists of duties and responsibilities. Not only are they valuable to the employee as complete summary of what his/her job entails, but they are also valuable to management. Both manager and employee will understand what to expect of the other. Management should design each job in a balanced way. This also helps in designing promotion paths and creating incentives. A typical job description should include the following topics:

- Purpose of position
- Duties and responsibilities

- Daily activities
- Supervisor
- Working hours
- Method and timing of evaluations and feedback

LEASES—COMMON TERMINOLOGY

Lease	A lease is a contract between lessor (the owner) and lessee (the tenant) whereby the lessor agrees to turn over to the lessee the right to use land, improvements, or both, in return for rent or other consideration.
Financial Lease	A financial lease is one that does not provide for service (maintenance), cannot be canceled, and is fully amortized. Fully amortized refers to the lessor receiving rental payments totaling the full price of the equipment lease plus interest over the term of the lease.
Net Lease	A lease in which the lessor pays for maintenance and taxes, and insurance.
Net Net Lease	The lessee agrees to pay some, but not all, of the maintenance, taxes, and insurance.
Net Net Net Lease	Sometimes referred to as a triple net lease, it is a lease in which the lessee pays all the maintenance, taxes, and insurance.
Percentage Lease	A lease which provides that a certain percentage of the lessee's gross sales will be the amount required for the periodic rent payment. This will usually be over and above a monthly minimum rate. A typical percentage lease for a food service operation runs about five to six percent of sales.

Sale/Leaseback   This type of transaction is a sale in which title passes from an individual or company making use of an asset to an investor, who then leases the asset back to the original owner, who continues to use the property as before.

LEGAL FORM OF ORGANIZATION

Since there are numerous factors involved in deciding which form of organization is best for your particular operation, the various advantages and disadvantages of each should be carefully weighed before any decision is made. Table 13 describes the most common forms of organization used in restaurants along with the advantages and disadvantages of each.

LIQUOR LICENSES

Any establishment that plans to sell liquor must obtain the appropriate license. The U.S. Bureau of Alcohol, Tobacco, and Firearms (ATF) regulates the manufacture and advertising of all alcoholic beverages.

There are many types of liquor licenses. In fact, the Department of Alcoholic Beverage Control (ABC in California—laws and regulating agencies vary from state to state) issues over fifty types of licenses, depending on the nature of the liquor and service offered. The licenses available can be generally classified under two categories: on-sale general public eating place licenses are issued to restaurants that serve cocktails, and on-sale general public premise licenses are issued to establishments which do not have to sell food but do sell a complete line of alcoholic beverages.

LOCATION

Location is a key element of your total business plan. Too often, not enough thought is given to such an important decision. Data that

TABLE 13

Legal Forms of Organization

TYPES	ADVANTAGES	DISADVANTAGES
SOLE PROPRIETORSHIP	Freedom of operation Profits retained in business (no dividends to others) Business losses deducted on personal income taxes Sole control of organization	All personal assets can be claimed to cover business debts Difficulty in acquiring capital for expansion Need for many personal abilities Sole burden of risk is on entrepreneur
THE PARTNERSHIP	More management input A variety of expertise available Additional capital sources Business gains and losses added or deducted on personal income taxes	Each partner is liable for all debts of the business (jointly and severally) Each partner is responsible for the obligations and contracts entered into by other partners Partnership automatically dissolved with death of a partner Some difficulty in attracting additional funds for expansion

TABLE 13 (Cont'd)

THE CORPORATION	Limited liability—maximum potential loss is the equity invested	Double taxation of income if dividends are paid
	Continuing existence—even upon death of a stockholder	Greater regulation—federal, state and local
	Capital easier to acquire	More types of taxation
	Transfer of ownership possible	Greater reporting required
	Possible separation of ownership and management	In a small corporation, limited liability is often circumvented by lenders who require personal guarantees on notes by the owners
SUBCHAPTER "S" CORPORATION (A hybrid partnership/corporation form of organization)	Limited liability	Only one class of stock allowed
	No double taxation of dividends	Up to 10 stockholders permitted—less capital available through additional stock sales
	Business gains and losses added or deducted on personal income taxes	

should be collected in order to make an intelligent decision about site location include:

- competition
- traffic count
- the types of businesses nearby (are they good generators of potential customers?)
- peak hours of traffic
- plans for growth in the area
- availability of public transportation
- parking facilities and ease of access
- the destinations of passers-by
- the number of residents within a given radius of the location
- visibility from adjacent stores and the road
- the average sales of competitors in the area
- other demographic data which is considered unique to your location

Your local real-estate agent or leasing agent can be of great assistance. They maintain up-to-date lists of available sites and demographic data on the area. Other sources of information include: the market research department of local newspapers, the chamber of commerce, the city planning office, and the local library.

There are many companies that specialize in site selection. With the aid of computer programs, much of the above information is recorded and cross-referenced with retrieval in the form of site profiles. The cost of these services can be very high and out of reach for the newcomer, but should be kept in mind for expansion in the future. Restaurant chains that are expanding operations should make use of these services. Chains that have existing computer facilities can use these programs on a time-sharing basis.

MANAGEMENT INFORMATION AND CONTROL SYSTEMS

Your accounting records are kept not only to determine how much money is owed in taxes each year. They also serve two other functions, called performance accounting and decision accounting.

Performance accounting measures the results of the restaurant operation in monetary terms. From these types of reports, a good manager can also extract information concerning food costs, labor costs, and labor productivity. These figures can then be measured against industry averages available through the National Restaurant Association, 311 First Street, N.W. Washington, D.C. 20001 or Laventhol and Horwath (certified public accountants who specialize in food service) to determine performance and costs that are out of line or those areas that need management attention.

Decision accounting provides management with quantitative information on which to base key management decisions (for example, decisions concerning menu pricing, advertising budgets, bonus plans, and menu mix). These types of reports can be derived from standard financial statements or from many of the new electronic cash register systems or point of sales (POS) systems that are currently available. Ask your accountant about break-even analysis, sales analysis, ratio analysis, and inventory control systems.

Many of the electronic cash registers can be programmed to supply the following management reports which are valuable in decision making.

- Sales analysis
- Menu mix analysis
- Labor productivity
- Time reports
- Peak hour reports
- Inventory control (perpetual)

Contact a local electronic cash-register dealer for a demonstration.

MARKET RESEARCH

Another aspect of marketing that is often overlooked by small business in general is market research. As simple as it is, it can be invaluable to the restaurateur.

The purpose of market research is to help determine the marketing strategy for a business. It is important that the restaurateur understand his/her customers' needs. So the marketing strategy should be designed not only to satisfy its customers' wants and needs but also to provide appropriate guidelines for employees. You may want to consult a market research firm or perform a limited project yourself.

A small project can provide the restaurateur with the answers to the following questions:

1. Where do individuals usually dine when they eat away from home?
2. Why do they eat there?
3. What is the market potential for your business?
4. How does your restaurant compare with the competition?
5. How effective is your advertising?
6. What products and services should you offer?

We will now illustrate how the answers to these questions can be obtained.

1. A simple question such as: "When you eat a meal away from home, which restaurant do you most often patronize?" will give you an idea of your current market position as well as the strength of your competition.

Table 14 represents the results of a questionnaire that was administered to 200 persons. The Fish Fantasy has about half the total market in this fictitious survey, and its greatest appeal is to young adults.

2. Why do customers patronize the place they do? There are several ways to get the answer to this question. One is to ask an "open-ended question" such as, "Why the Fish Fantasy?" Answers will usually fall into a few categories such as quality, convenience, price, etc. Another approach is often called "forced importance rating." When customers are asked to order a list of qualities such as those mentioned, a sorting takes place which will help you determine key elements.

TABLE 14

Market Position*

	Fish Fantasy	Johnny D's	Lobster Haven	Hawaiian Palace
Sex:				
Male	55	29	5	22
Female	42	25	7	15
TOTAL	97	54	12	37
Age:				
18-24	10	15	0	0
25-34	38	20	3	4
35-44	25	11	5	6
45-64	15	8	3	24
65-over	9	0	1	3
TOTAL	97	54	12	37
Income:				
Under $7,000	12	13	0	0
$7,000-$14,999	15	30	4	2
$15,000-$24,999	40	6	7	9
$25,000-over	30	5	1	26
TOTAL	97	54	12	37
Children at Home:				
0	00	33	5	2
1	27	16	2	5
2	31	4	3	8
3	22	1	2	16
4	15	0	0	4
5 +	2	0	0	2
TOTAL	97	54	12	37
% of TOTAL Respondents	49%	27%	6%	18%

*Numbers in table represent number of respondents except where noted.

3. What is your market potential? The following questions can be asked to determine potential by time period:

- "Within the last month, how many times have you visited a full-service restaurant?"
- At what time of day do you usually patronize these restaurants?"

4. How does your restaurant compare with its competition? It is important to discover the strengths of your competitors and to compare your business to theirs. To accomplish this, various questions may be asked: "How would you compare the Fish Fantasy and Restaurant B with regard to the following factors?" The factors used should include friendliness, cleanliness, value, and quality.

5. Advertising Effectiveness. It is important to determine the impact advertising has on prospective customers. To do this, a question such as, "Have you read, seen, or heard any advertising lately for the Fish Fantasy Restaurant?" may be asked. A good follow-up would be, "What would be the best way to inform you with an advertisement about a special or new product?" You could then test for image or character by asking the respondent to identify a slogan or logo.

6. Services. Market research can also make it possible for you to discover if additional services are desired by your customers. An open-ended question can be asked to determine these types of needs: "What would you suggest the Fish Fantasy do to improve its operation?"

An introductory statistics book will provide valuable information on sample design and data analysis. Only by understanding market research and its results will you be able to meet the needs of your customers, plan effective strategies, and have a good basis for decision making.

PERMITS, TAXES, REGISTRATIONS

- Liquor Licenses—Covered in a separate section. See page 92.

- Seller's Permit—Issued by the State Board of Equalization, this requires a fixed fee. A deposit is usually required based on a percentage of projected taxable sales.

- Permit to Operate—Issued by the local health department after inspection of the operation. Fees vary.

- Retail Liquor Dealers Stamp—Obtained from the IRS or the U.S. Bureau of Alcohol, Tobacco & Firearms.

- Employer's Identification Number (EI)—This number is issued by the IRS to be used when submitting federal income and social security taxes withheld from employees' wages and when paying the tax mentioned above.

- Property Taxes—They are imposed annually on the unit's inventory and equipment by the city or county assessor's office.

- Fictitious Name Registration—This must be filed with the county clerk and advertised in a local publication of general circulation.

- Business License—This license is available at either the county courthouse or the city hall. The license must be openly displayed.

- Fire Clearance—This is issued after inspection by the local fire department. The fee is small, and this permit must also be openly displayed.

PERSONNEL

Availability

Turnover in this industry is a continual problem for managers. Be aware that it does exist. Also consider the various places from which necessary labor can be drawn. Where can the restaurant meet its labor needs?

Fast food restaurants rely heavily on high-school and young

college students. This is primarily due to the less sophisticated tasks to be performed and the fact that most young people will work for minimum wage. This is one reason labor cost, as a percentage of sales, is lower for fast food establishments than those with full service. Full-service restaurants require a more stable group of employees, especially trained cooks. Hence, the labor cost is bound to be higher.

An ideal place to look for personnel is at the local high schools and/or colleges. Typically, the schools will advertise job opportunities for free. For attracting full-time help, local newspapers provide an effective medium. If you feel that you can afford the price, experienced help is always preferable. However, you must offer an opportunity attractive enough to pull them away from a current job.

Compensation and Benefits

Although compensation is an important ingredient in acquiring and maintaining personnel, it is not the only ingredient. Nontangible things such as job satisfaction, positive feedback, and evaluation of work performance are equally important. Prudent managers remember that employees are not motivated by money alone.

Salary should be competitive with other restaurants in the area. Ask employees what they are making at other establishments. Another way is to check classified ads for such information. Restaurant associations are also a good source of wage information.

Benefits vary widely from restaurant to restaurant. Generally, chains offer more in this area because of their size and resources. Considerations in this area include:

Meals   Will employees be charged for meals? How much? How many meals per shift are allowed? Most common in the trade is to allow employees meals at one-half the menu price.

Vacations Full-time personnel are concerned with vacations and generally receive two weeks after one year of service.

Part-time help after one year of work may receive a prorated share of two weeks based on the number of hours worked.

Sick Pay   This area varies widely also. The only generalization that can be made here is that part-time help is usually not eligible for such benefits.

Insurance Health and dental plans are usually found in restaurant chains and are on a contributory basis. Independents sometimes offer a type of health plan to key employees such as cooks and management personnel.

Uniforms There is no real consensus in this area whether employees buy their own uniforms or whether they are supplied by the restaurant. However, don't expect employees to be too eager to buy uniforms. Make the cooks and dishroom personnel uniforms simple and comfortable. Service personnel uniforms should be attractive, comfortable, and easy to clean. In many states it is required that the employer offer a uniform allowance for the cleaning of required uniforms.

Performance Reviews

Periodic performance reviews of all employees are an effective way to achieve better performance and/or improve management's rapport with employees. This is an opportunity to invite employees' comments and suggestions and allow the management to give feedback to them on their job performance. This is generally done at six-month intervals. Compensation reviews are usually annual.

PLANNING AND TIMING

Planning and timing are very important with almost any new business. Sometimes referred to as a business plan, your restaurant proposal is an example of planning. You must exercise good timing in order to carry out your plan in the most efficient and effective manner. Efficient means at the least cost, and effective means getting the plan implemented and accomplished. A little extra effort now to insure good timing can save you many dollars in the future. A very helpful tool in timing the implementation of your plan is called the Program Evaluation and Review Technique (or PERT Chart). It will help you visualize the many steps involved and the way they fit together to reach your final goal—the opening of your restaurant. A PERT Chart is a flow chart of the steps involved in your restaurant development, i.e., what must be done, and when, in order to complete and open the operation.

POLICIES AND PROCEDURES

Every restaurant should have a Policies and Procedures Manual. While these manuals vary widely, they cover all the salient points that must be implemented if an organization is to function effectively. Table 15 illustrates a typical table of contents for a Policies and Procedures Manual (also called the Organization Manual or Operations Manual).

SECURITY

Security problems include robbery and employee pilferage. Extreme losses due to robbery can be deterred by depositing cash daily, and by keeping extra cash in a safe, not in the register.

Employee pilferage is a common problem in the restaurant industry. These types of thefts are difficult to detect, especially if the owner does not work the unit himself. Your method of preventing employee pilferage should be consistent with your style of management. For example, an owner or manager who wants to build employee trust and open channels of communication, and who has developed profit-sharing plans and bonus systems should realize there will be negative reactions to installing overhead television cameras in storage rooms and walk-ins.

TABLE 15

Sample Outline of an Operations Manual
Fish Fantasy Policies & Procedures
Table of Contents

Implementing strict control systems is another answer. Allow only one person access to a given storeroom and give that person responsibility for its contents. Although it reduces pilferage, it has the disadvantages of promoting inefficiency, inconvenience, and maybe some animosity among the staff. This is one aspect of restaurant management for which there is no textbook answer. It's up to your creativity, rapport with the employees, and management style.

USING PROFESSIONAL SERVICES EFFECTIVELY

Professional services can be the best investment any organization will make. If used correctly, the cost/benefit ratio of legal, accounting, banking, and insurance professionals is extremely favorable. It should be remembered, however, that these services can be extremely costly and care must be taken to use them efficiently.

In your business plan you have already defined your overall need for professional services. If you are adequately prepared you will be able to converse effectively and succinctly with lawyers, accountants, and the like, and accurately prepare them so that they can fill your needs. Knowing what you want before you visit these people can save hundreds of dollars and increase your understanding of their advice. Know what questions to ask. Know your options, but don't make the mistake of trying to do everything yourself. Concentrate on the restaurant operation—that is your expertise.

The Professional Talent Pool

The best way to save money on professional services is to do your homework. You do not necessarily save money by finding someone to do it cheap. Seek the talents of someone who is familiar with restaurants, particularly start-up situations. Avoid using relatives, if possible, simply because it is not likely that restaurant start-ups are their specialty. One hour with a top-notch lawyer or accountant may be worth as much as several hours or days with an inexperienced professional.

Bankers

These professionals are very good people to become acquainted with, even if you are not presently seeking money. Inevitably, one must use the services of a bank. Such matters as checking, deposit of receipts, and other daily business matters involve banks. Find a bank that makes you comfortable. By all means, introduce yourself to one of the lending officers and the bank manager if possible. Tell them of your venture and your overall business plan. If some time in the future you discover a need for short-term financing or longer term debt for expansion, chances are they will be receptive to your request.

A good relationship with a banker is essential. Often banks can be of much more assistance to a small business than is realized. However, no one likes lending money to a stranger, so the relationship should be developed early. First of all, seek a banker that has an interest in small business. Often certain branches of a large bank specialize in small business. There are branches or banks that specialize in real estate, S.B.A. loans, etc., while others won't consider them.

When you present a loan package to a banker, even if you did not prepare it, make sure that you can discuss it. You must develop a sense of your own competence in the banker's mind; one of the quickest ways to lose it is to present a plan you don't understand yourself. How much will your rent cost? How did you compute your depreciation? What are the terms of your lease? You should be capable of providing input to your loan package (proposal).

Remember, lenders are in the business of selling money and services, and generally desire to maintain an ongoing relationship with business. They, too, have their eye on the long-term needs of your organization. Therefore, do not hesitate to seek their services when needed. Bank services include:

1. *Business Advice*—on important business decisions affecting your company.
2. *Credit Advice*—the company's credit as well as suppliers.

3. *Agency Services*—trusts, collections, and disbursements.
4. *Safe Deposit Boxes*—safekeeping of corporate records.

Certified Public Accountants

A C.P.A. is necessary for all businesses, particularly those that have more than just the entrepreneur financially involved. Banks and other lenders usually require certified financial statements while a loan is outstanding, and often before a loan is granted. Investors usually desire similar treatment, particularly if they represent absentee ownership

Do not view accountants as necessary evils, but rather as professionals who can provide great assistance to a growing concern. Some auxiliary services that C.P.A.'s provide include:

1. *Tax Planning*—essential for a growing business.
2. *Auditing*—to certify financial statements.
3. *Consulting*—in particular EDP consulting and advice on implementing your own computer system. However, three or more units would be required before the cost of a C.P.A. *consultant* is justified.

Insurance Brokers

This is a service vital to any business. See the section on this subject on page 87.

Lawyers

There are many legal aspects to starting any new business, particularly the highly regulated restaurant industry. Developing a good relationship with a lawyer in advance of any crisis is good business. Also, reliance on a good lawyer puts less burden on management and allows more time for daily operations. More specifically, lawyers can aid in:

1. Deciding which form of organization is best for your situation.
2. Developing important contacts with financial institutions and various government agencies.
3. Handling all legal aspects of starting your business.
4. Personal planning.

TRADE ASSOCIATIONS

Trade associations can be very helpful in developing a restaurant concept and proposal. Most associations maintain very complete libraries and stay abreast of trends and current legislation affecting the industry. Below is a list of associations which may be very helpful.

National Restaurant Association (NRA)
Main office
311 First Street, N.W.
Washington, D.C. 20001
Chicago office
7 IBM Plaza, Suite 2600
Chicago, IL 60611
(The NRA will supply addresses of state restaurant associations.)

National Licensed Beverage Association
1025 Vermont Ave., N.W., Suite 601
Washington, D.C. 20005

International Franchise Association, Inc.
333 North Michigan Avenue
Chicago, IL 60601

National Small Business Association
301-1225 15th St., N.W.
Washington, D.C. 20036

American Management Association
135 W. 50th Street
New York, NY 10020

TRADE JOURNALS

Trade journals are the best source of timely, specialized information of concern to the food service operator. Issues typically cover new product ideas, convention calendars, marketing strategies, energy-saving tips, and market surveys and forecasts. Below is a list of available food service journals.

Cornell Hotel & Restaurant Administration Quarterly
School of Hotel Administration
Cornell University
Ithaca, NY 14850

Restaurant Hospitality
614 Superior Avenue West
Cleveland, OH 44113

Food Service Marketing
2132 Fordem Avenue Box 7158
Madison, WI 53707

Institutions/Volume Feeding Magazine
5 South Wabash Avenue
Chicago, IL 60603

Nation's Restaurant News
425 Park Avenue
New York, NY 10022

Restaurant Business
633 Third Avenue
New York, NY 10017

Western Food Service
1709 West Eighth Street
Los Angeles, CA 90017

Beverage Industry News
703 Market Street
San Francisco, CA 94103

Beverage Bulletin
8383 Wilshire Boulevard
Beverly Hills, CA 90211

SUGGESTED READING

Profitable Restaurant Management
by Kenneth Solomon and Norman Katz
Prentice-Hall, Inc.
Englewood Cliffs, NJ 07092

How to Manage a Restaurant or Institutional Food Service
by John W. Stokes
Wm. C. Brown Company, Publishers
Dubuque, IA

Designing Restaurant Interiors: A Guide for Food Service Operators, by Harry Backus, A.S.I.D.
Lebhar-Friedman Books
New York, NY 10022

How to Organize and Operate a Small Business
by Clifford Baumback, Kenneth Lawyer, and Pearce Kelley
Prentice-Hall, Inc.
Englewood Cliffs, NJ 07092

Up Your Own Organization
by Donald M. Dible
The Entrepreneur Press
Santa Clara, CA 95051

INDEX

Registrations, 99-100
Retail liquor dealers stamp, 100

Sale/leaseback, 92
Sales forecast, 18, 19
Security, 103-105
Seller's permit, 99-100
Small Business Reporter, 81
Special multiperil program
    (SMP) insurance, 89

Taxes, 99-100
Timing, 102-103

Trade associations, 108
Trade journals, 109-110
Triple net lease, 91

Uniform Commercial Code, Section 6-102 of, 76-77
U.S. Bureau of Alcohol, Tobacco, and Firearms (ATF), 92

Workers' compensation insurance, 87